AF265589

EIGHT SHORT STORIES

EIGHT
SHORT STORIES

BY

LENNOX ROBINSON

DUBLIN
The Talbot Press Ltd.
89 Talbot Street

LONDON
T. Fisher Unwin Ltd.
1 Adelphi Terrace

CONTENTS

THE RETURN

Iт had rained heavily all day, and a cold,
damp wind was blowing down the platform.
The train was already late and would be later,
I was told. I made up my mind to at least
an hour's delay, and began to walk up and
down to keep myself warm. The platform
was crowded with people : with ordinary
travellers, with faimers and their wives
returning from a market, with the strings of
girls with arms linked and the groups of
young men who crowd the railway stations
in the evening in Ireland, and it was five
or ten minutes before I caught sight of the
little group which has filled my thoughts
ever since.

It consisted of three persons, a woman and
two men. It was the woman who attracted
my attention first. She was young—not
more than twenty, perhaps, but quite mature.
She had black hair and beautiful eyes, and
the soft, rich line of her cheek and chin
recalled that mixture of purity and sensuous-

B

ness one sees so often in the Madonnas of the early Italian painters. It was a type of face not very often seen among Irish peasant girls, and I stayed near her, watching with keen pleasure the slow, graceful movements of her head. The black shawl made a perfect frame for the picture. The man beside her—her husband, evidently—was a less fine creature. Tall and awkward, with an anxious, bewildered expression, he kept on enquiring of passing porters why the train was so late and whether they were on the right platform. The woman, on the contrary, stood with a kind of sad patience, and at her companion's restlessness and the porters' hasty replies would slowly smile, and then her face would again sink back into its sad, sensuous beauty. Presently a guard pushed up to her a luggage truck and, helped by her husband, she sat down on it and then took from under her shawl the two crutches which had supported her and which I had not noticed.

The third member of the group stood a little apart and did not, I think, belong to them. He was short, with a broad un-Irish face ; a large silver medal was on his breast, and on the ground beside him stood a strange-looking bottle enclosed in a straw basket, and a small bag such as country folk going to America carry. He was evidently blind, and he stood there in perfect quiesence clasping a stick, with his head held high in a listening attitude. The late train, the crowded platform, did not interest him at all. He had the immense patience of the blind.

Up to this no one had taken any notice of the little group, but now a priest began to talk to the blind man, and immediately the bored listeners surged round and I moved farther away. The man's strange face, the foreign-looking jar, made me think that perhaps he was a foreigner, and if so I did not want to be one of that discourteous, inquisitive crowd. The priest talked to him for a long time, and then he too went away ; but still a group of people were gathered round the blind man, craning, gaping, questioning. But now and then I caught a glimpse of him in the same attitude as before, clasping his stick, his head thrown back, his patient, expressionless face.

When the train did arrive—an hour late —I found myself in the same carriage as the priest. After a station or two the other people in the carriage got out, and I moved across and sat down beside him.

" Was that man on the platform quite blind, Father ? " I asked.

" Indeed he was. Stone blind."

" He wasn't a foreigner ? "

" Oh no. They were coming back from Lourdes."

The roar of the train had caught the last words, and I hardly heard them.

" They were what ? "

" They were coming home from Lourdes."

When I realised what he had said there came over me a rush of pity, almost a sort of horror, and I could say no more.

.   .   .   .   .

The priest got out at the next station, the rain beat on the glass, the cold wind blew through the badly-fitting door, and in imagination I saw the whole progression of facts.

First, there was the vague idea, the unspoken wish, then the suggestion by a neighbour or by the husband " If herself could only go to Lourdes maybe she'd be cured. . . ." At first it was thought an impossible idea— where was the money to come from ? .Then later, " Well, maybe we might manage it." And then began the scraping together of the money ; perhaps the neighbours helped, perhaps the priest helped, somehow or other at last the money was gathered. Not much need be spent on new clothes, not much luggage need be taken, but as the time for departure approached the days must have succeeded each other in a crescendo of excitement. Then at last the great day arrives; probably the cottage they live in is up among the hills; there is a long drive to the railway station, a journey in a slow stopping train, a change to a fast train, other pilgrims are in it; then comes the steamer, then another train—an express this time, and so on—quicker—quicker—on—on to Lourdes.

One can imagine the facts of the journey so clearly. But that other progression, that crescendo of spiritual feeling—it is not so easy to guess at it. That it was intense and deep cannot be questioned. For these people that journey to Lourdes was no mere tourist trip flavoured with religion, it was a pilgrimage of soul and body; and the prayers in Ireland and the prayers in Lourdes, the prayers on the train, the prayers on the steamer—what a chain they made! It must have seemed as if the miracle was accomplished before ever Lourdes was reached; the hands must have loosened on those crutches, those eyes must have quickened with eagerness.

Something in one's heart forbids one to go any further. At the sight of those blinded eyes, those crutches, still, alas! so necessary, one is in the presence of a tragedy too poignant to be analysed and probed. The realisation of failure may have been sudden or gradual, it may have come in rebellion or resignation. Let us pass over it quickly to the little patient group on the draughty sodden platform.

Ah! the diminuendo of that return, the exhaustion after the exaltation, the train getting slower and slower, no crowds of excited people at the stations, only blank indifference or a curiosity more galling still. The return to the little cottage, the old life that must be taken up ; for the man the same darkness, for the woman the same pain. . . .

I tried to tell myself that my imagination had run away with me, that the journey had been an interest and excitement and that the disappointment would soon be forgotten, and that—for the woman, at any rate—the strange foreign sights would be a rich memory for the rest of her life. I almost persuaded myself that it was best as it was.

·   ·   ·   ·   ·

It was nearly midnight when the train reached the terminus. It was still raining, and I stumbled, stiff and cold, out of my carriage on the platform.

At the carriage door next to mine the tall man was standing, and in the doorway stood the woman. She stretched out her arms and put them around his neck, and with great tenderness he lifted her to the ground. Over his shoulder I saw her head from which the shawl had slipped back and for an instant my eyes met hers—pure, sensuous, infinitely patient.

October, 1912.

THE FACE

NEVER in the daytime or in bright sunlight could you see it, but sometimes just before sunset when some sinking ray of the sun was reflected from the rock to the lake's dark surface, and always in moonlight and on clear starry nights then, lying flat on the top of the cliff and peering over you could see the face quite clearly.

It lay in the deep pool at the foot of the cliff, a few yards from the shore and apparently a foot or two deep in the water. First it appeared as a piece of white rock with a film of lakeweed floating across it, then gradually your vision cleared and you saw the pale features distinctly, the closed eyes and the long dark lashes, the curved eyebrows, the gentle mouth and the fair hair which half hid the white neck and which sometimes drifted like a veil across the face; below the neck the pool lay in deeper shadow, and no one had ever been able to tell the shape of the beautiful creature that lay there.

It was a precipitous climb down the face of the cliff and no one but Jerry Sullivan had ventured it, but as he touched with his fingers the water of the pool the face shivered away, and stretching his arm deep into the water it met nothing except a tendril of lake-weed. Only once had he climbed down because he was afraid that if he probed too deeply the face would disappear for ever—for it was days after he touched the water before he saw it again; for the future he was content to gaze at it from above.

He had known it all his life. He could not have been more than six years old when his father had led him to the cliff's edge and shown him the sleeping face in the water. He had never been afraid of it as were some of the other boys, on the contrary when he was sent to drive the sheep from one hill to another he would contrive to pass the lake either coming or going, he would loiter there until the sun sank and risk a scolding when he got home; but hardly a week passed without his seeing the face.

Up among those lonely mountains he saw few women. There was only his mother, old now and grey, and a mile or two to the west the MacCarthy's cottage with the two girls

Peg and Ellen, coarsely featured both with thick black hair, and the few other women he saw from time to time were either coarsely dark or foxy red. Was it any wonder that he turned from them to the fair face floating in the water ? any wonder that as he grew older he judged every woman's face by that hard standard and found them all wanting.

His father died when he was eighteen years old and Jerry lived on with his mother, tilling the little bit of land, cutting turf on the side of the mountain, driving the sheep. It was a lonely, silent life—for he was an only child—and his mother often urged him to take a wife, but he made the excuse that while she was there he wanted no other woman in the house, and though she remonstrated with him she was well content to remain sole mistress of the cottage to the day of her death. He never told her of those hours he spent by the lake ; hidden in a fold of the hills no one saw him go there, the neighbours shunned the place as haunted, and as the years crept by the face grew to be more and more particularly his own.

Fifteen years after his father's death his mother died, and when the funeral was over he climbed the mountain and stared for a long time into the water. It was a stormy winter evening and as the sun went down a pale young moon appeared. Never had the face been so clear, never had it looked more lovely. He had felt very lonely when the earth was thrown on his mother's coffin, now he felt quietly content. He had nothing left in the world to love except this face. It had no rival now, he could pour out all the love of his heart in adoration of it.

And so for three years it went on like this : more and more he shunned the neighbours, more and more time he spent by the lake. He began to neglect the farm, for what pleasure was there in working only for himself ? and to the overtures of the matchmakers he was either morosely silent or roughly violent. He spent now whole nights on the cliff; sometimes he thought he saw a stirring of the eyelids and the fancy grew in him that after sufficient concentration of devotion on his part the eyes would open ; already the cheeks seemed less pale, the mouth had parted slightly, he thought he saw a gleam of white teeth.

He grew worn with watching. The woman in the water seemed to draw her vitality from him, and as her cheeks grew fuller his own, grew thin, and as her face flushed his paled until one evening gazing down at those closed eyes he saw the lids stir and stir again and at last very slowly they opened. The eyes behind them were dazzlingly blue and they met his grey ones with a long comprehending look. Everything he had ever hoped to see in a woman's eyes was there, and half in terror, half in joy, he gave a cry and drew back from the cliff; when he looked again a second later the face had vanished.

He thought he would see it the next night, but he looked in vain. He was frantic. There had been weeks before when on account of the weather or some trick of light he had been unable to see the face, but always through those dark days he had been conscious that it was waiting for him in the water, ready to re-appear at any moment; now he was only conscious of a great blank, an emptiness, a desolation. He ran round the lake like a distracted man, he looked into other pools—in vain. With the opening of her eyes she had fled and the little lake was as deserted as a last year's nest.

It was three days later at the fair of Coolmore that he found her. She was standing with her back to the wall outside the post-office, and a little curious crowd was round her questioning her and touching her clothes. There was a strangeness, a foreignness about her, and when the village policeman came and began to question her the crowd gathered closer, but her replies were incoherent ; she did not know her name or where she had come from or where she was going ; she stood there lonely and aloof and her blue eyes kept searching every face piteously, like a blind man feeling with his stick for the pavement's edge. Then she lifted her eyes and beyond the fringe of the crowd they met Jerry's eyes. He again saw that look, he strode to her pushing the crowd away roughly to right and left, he put his arm into hers and led her to his house.

The priest married them and they lived in perfect contentment and happiness. She had been pale and fragile when he brought her home, but she grew every day stronger and more beautiful. She knew nothing of housework or farmwork and learned but little, preferring to sit in the shadow of a rock in the field while Jerry worked and in the winter to crouch in the corner near the fire or sit in the window in the moonlight. He was quite content to have her so and gladly did the work of two ; he liked the mystery of her, he liked to feel her different from the neighbours. She never could tell him where she came from and he soon ceased to question her ; he told her of the face in the water, but it seemed to awaken no memory in her mind, and yet sometimes, looking at her—especially when she sat in the moonlight—the texture of her body would seem to become fluidic, her face would appear as if floating, and behind it he would seem to see that other face with its closed eyes. That face had disappeared from the lake and he never went to the cliff now.

In the second November after their marriage when the moon was full a child was born to them, a child as fragile as a moon-ray, that lay in the cradle hardly stirring, never crying.

The fair of Coolmore was held ten days later and Jerry had to bring some cattle to it to sell. Coolmore lay fifteen miles away across the mountain, and he got up very early in the morning, lit the fire, left food and drink for his wife, and started. Peg Mac-Carthy had promised to look in at her once or twice during the day and he knew she would want for nothing.

He sold his cattle, but there was a delay about payment and it was after four o'clock when he left Coolmore village. He walked quickly, the money was heavy in his pocket, his mind was strangely anxious about his wife and he made the best pace he could. The evening grew colder and colder, yellowish-grey clouds came up from the north-east, the rushes in the lonely bogs bent to the wind, and as he reached the top of the pass it began to snow. It was early in the year for snow, but this was a heavy shower and the big flakes half blinded him as he pushed doggedly on. But his boots grew clogged, he had to walk more and more slowly, and when he was three miles from home he determined to take a short cut across the hills which would shorten his road by half a mile. It was wild walking but he knew every foot of the path, it led him along the top of the cliff above the lake, and he stopped for a minute there to get his breath. The snow had ceased to fall, the sky was clearing, a few stars shone out and the lake lay black at his feet. Something— old habit perhaps—made him fall on his knees and peer over, and there in the pool below he saw the face. It was there just as it had always been with closed eyes and floating hair. He rose to his feet vaguely troubled. He had never seen it since his marriage.

Half a mile from his house he met Peg MacCarthy walking quickly towards him. " Thank God it's yourself, Jerry " she said. " The wife, God help me, is gone. I saw her just before milking time and she was sitting by the fire; I said you'd have a bad walk home and she said she wished she could go and meet you; then afterwards, and I sitting at my tea, a step passed on the road and now when I went to your house she's gone."

Hardly stopping to answer her he ran home. It was true, she was not there. The child lay quietly sleeping in its cradle. Then he thought of the face in the lake and he ran up the road and along the path and over the breast of the hill to the cliff's edge. The face was there still, and again as he had done years before he climbed down to the rock. He still saw the face, he touched the water, the face did not vanish, he plunged in his arms and drew his wife's body to the shore.

In the water the face had appeared living, out of it with the wet hair clinging about it it was cold and dead. Had she come to meet him and fallen in ? He could see no hurt on her. Or had she fled from him back to the element to which she belonged ? The wet form in his arms seemed less his than' the woman in the water. Every impulse of his nature urged him to lay her back. He did so and she sank in the deep pool till only her face was seen.

He climbed the cliff and walked home. He felt strangely bewildered. He hardly grieved. Had he lost her or had he ever had her ? Was this only the evening of his mother's funeral and had he, kneeling on that cliff, fallen into a dream and dreamed of the face's awakening, of the marriage, of the child ? No, this last was real at any rate, and he took it from the cradle and held it in his arms and stood by the window looking out at the dying moon. And yet—was it only fancy—or, as the sickly moon sank did the child really grow lighter and lighter in his arms, and would he find when morning broke that he was only clasping a tangle of wet lake-weed wrapped in an old quilt ?

November, 1913.

LOOKING AFTER THE GIRLS

Mrs. O'Riordan stood at the farmhouse door and looked down the road.

"What's keeping them girls?" she said to herself.

From the road her eyes wandered to the cornfield below the house, tinged now with green—for it was late April—and from the cornfield to the two meadows and beyond to the fields of potatoes and mangolds and across the little river to the rich pasture land. Ten milking cows were driven through the yard under her eyes as she stood there, and she watched them with anxious approval.

"Everything's looking well, thanks be to God," she murmured; "but them girls will want it, every penny."

It was not a large farm, hardly a hundred and fifty acres; but the land was rich and sheltered, lying in an airy valley between low hills, which protected it on the north and east and left it open to the south and west. A small river curled round the hill and supplied

water for the cattle even during the driest
summer. It was a " warm farm," as the
County Cork people say, and when James
O'Riordan died of the fever it was felt that,
apart from his personal loss, his widow need
be little pitied.

" I don't know, then," she'd say in reply to
the half-congratulatory condolences of her
neighbours ; " five girls is a terrible troop to
get married out of a small place like this, and
I wouldn't be wishing any of them to die
single or to have to go to America."

The troop had turned the corner now and
were coming up the road, their satchels of
school-books on their shoulders. Katty, the
eldest, was just sixteen, and Teresa, the
youngest, dragging at her arm, was hardly
six.

" Robert," Mrs. O'Riordan called, " bring
in a sup of fresh milk for the girls' tea."

Robert came out of the cowshed, carrying
a small pail of milk. He was six years older
than Katty, and the graves of his two brothers
filled the gap between them.

" Here it is, mother."

He stood for a moment beside her at the
door. " Katty's growing in a fright," he
said.

" She is then: Oh, Robert, I pray to God to give me health and strength to look after them poor fatherless girls."

Robert laid his hand on her arm. He was tall and grave, full of a kind of patient strength, and for a moment she felt as if the dead James stood beside her.

But her prayers fell on deaf ears, for three months later she died.

" Look after them poor girls," she implored Robert almost with her last breath. " Get suitable matches for them. I know you'll be the same as a father to them. Oh, my poor girls ! "

" I will, mother ; I will," he said.

.   .   .   .   .

And indeed no father could have done more for his children than did Robert for those five sisters. They had free education ; clothes were not a serious consideration. The great crisis, the great test in each girl's career and the test of Robert's capacity as their guardian, was their marriage.

Katty, to be sure, was disposed of easily enough, and within three years of her mother's death ; but she was handsome and quick-spoken, and dazzled a little by the good match she was making—she married a young horse-dealer—Robert was lavish with the marriage settlement, and was easily outmanœuvred by the bridegroom, who, of course, was an adept at bargaining for live-stock. When the question of Julia's marriage came up, a couple of years later, Robert realised bitterly how dearly he would have to pay for his extravagance with Katty, and how his sisters' marriages were going to burden and cripple him.

For since his father's death his own personal freedom was gone. Not until the last of his sisters was settled down could he think of his own future. Even if he had made no promise to his mother, it would have been difficult for him to marry while his sisters were still with him, but with the dying woman's words always in his ears, it became impossible, and he resolutely put aside that hope he had had of marrying Mary Shea, and he danced at her wedding with as light a step as he could.

But he began to realise that it took years and money to marry off his sisters. After months of bargaining Julia's match was broken off because he could not offer enough to please her future father-in-law, and Julia —embittered and resentful—remained in the house as an active spur and reminder to him of his duties and failings. He now applied himself desperately to the work of the farm, he rose early and worked late, saved here and scraped there, and was able to get the third girl—Maggie—satisfactorily married eleven years after his mother's death.

Maggie's marriage portion had impoverished him, but he thought he could count on a few years to recoup himself before either Bridget or Teresa need be expected to marry. But five years of disaster, disease, and bad harvest fell on the farm, and to marry Bridget he had to borrow from the bank and sell two cows.

And then six months later a great match turned up for Teresa. It would have been criminal to have hesitated—the worst treachery to his dead mother and father. The young man had come back from America, heir to his uncle's farm, which adjoined Robert's ; and by slicing off a few fields, and borrowing a little more from the bank, the match was arranged and the marriage took place.

Only Julia now was left ; Julia, embittered nd eed, but by no means despairing of getting a match. But she looked high—as high as her sisters, or higher. She was not going to be " given away with a threepenny-bit," she scornfully said ; and for ten years her nagging, bitter tongue kept him company across the fire at night and echoed in his ears as he went round the fields all day. By grinding toil that was permanently wearing out his body, by constant anxieties that lined his forehead and wearied his mind, he had succeeded in paying off the bank, and slowly the savings were beginning to accumulate again. Across his path now there came a girl—she seemed twin sister to the Mary Shea of his early dreams—and he found himself longing with a passionate eagerness for Julia's marriage, for an empty house to which he might bring that girl, for a soft voice at his fireside instead of that nagging one, for little children playing about.

Julia's choice fell on a hard-headed cattle-dealer, who had lost his first wife and wanted someone to look after the public-house which was such a useful asset to his trade. There was not a glimmer of romance about the matter, it was all harsh business, and the cattle-dealer named a sum as the fortune he expected so stupendous that Robert could only declare it utterly impossible. Then came from Julia recriminations, scourging words, tears, tempers; a slight relaxation of terms on the cattle-dealer's side, more pressure from Julia, ceaseless nagging.

" But sure the money isn't there—no, nor half of it," he cried despairingly.

" Well, if it comes to that, maybe I'd take a couple of the fields near the town; they'd do for grazing."

Robert demurred.

" You gave thirty acres away with Teresa. Would you grudge me a miserable field ? " Julia flashed at him.

It was much more than a field—in fact, the cattle-dealer seemed to want nearly half his farm; but because he had had too many years of Julia's bitterness, and because that other girl was always in his thoughts, he yielded suddenly and gave in on every point.

So the last of the girls was married, and when at the marriage party he saw the happy faces of the five sisters round the table, and their husbands and children, he felt his work fulfilled and completed, and the driving force that had urged him on all these years suddenly failed him; the glass in his hand slipped from his fingers, and he fell heavily to the ground.

He lay in hospital for ten weeks, sleeping and eating simply, like a child, asking no questions. Then when June came they told him he was well again and sent him home.

He did not reach the farm till evening, and after he had had his tea he walked out to the haggard and leaned against the gate. All the scents of June came from the meadow beside him ; the corncrakes called and answered from field to field.   He had never felt so light-hearted and young ; for the first time in his life he was absolutely free, free to marry Mary Flynn, free to scatter or to save.

And then, as chance would have it, Mary Flynn herself came up the lane. He bid her good-night as she passed, and she stopped.

" I'm glad to see you back again, Mr. O'Riordan," she said. " Sure the place hasn't been the same at all without you. I hope you've got your health again."

" I have, then, Mary, I have."

" But sure it must be very lonely for you about in the house with Julia gone and all. But, indeed, I suppose you'll be looking for a wife yourself next."

She would have passed on with a laugh, but he stopped her.

" That's just what I've been thinking," he

blundered. "If yourself and myself were to get married—would you, Mary . . . ?"

"Yerra! get on now, Mr. O'Riordan," she laughed back at him; "stop your joking!"

It was no joke, he insisted; he was in earnest, deadly earnest; he loved her, had loved her for years, ever since he was a boy; and he caught her by the arm, pouring out a torrent of words that half confused, half frightened the girl.

"Let go, will you? Let go! Is it me marry an old fellow like you? How dare you say you loved me all your life when I've heard my mother saying you courted her five-and-twenty years ago!"

But before she broke away from him he kissed her; kissed her as a boy of twenty would have kissed her; kissed her as he would have kissed her mother, Mary Shea, a quarter of a century ago.

"You shameless old man," she screamed, "with your grey head and your three fields and your broken-down house, to ask the like of me to be your wife! Sure there's not a girl in the country would have you! You'll have to go look for someone as old and broken as yourself—you shameless old man!"

Perhaps he was still weak from his illness,

for he remained leaning against the gate for a long time after she had left him, the words she had spoken moving dully round and round in his brain. He laughed a quavering laugh.

"The bitter things young girls do be saying!" he said to himself as he walked back to the house.

At the door he paused and looked at the farm which was spread out below him. He was surprised to see the meadows beyond the road were cut and the hay lying in swathes for he had been told at tea that none of his hay had yet been cut. Then he remembered: those fields were Julia's now, and the fields beyond them again, and Teresa had that big square of ground to the right. There was truth in the girl's bitter words: the best of his farm was gone.

The kitchen was deserted; the slatternly servant was out gossiping with a neighbour; the tea-things remained unwashed on the table. He decided to go to bed.

"The bitter words of a young girl!" he muttered as he groped his way upstairs.

And then in his room he found himself face to face with a man—a man with grey hair, a lined face, and hollow, tired eyes, who stared at him out of a glass.

" My God ! " he said, and put up his hand to his hair, and the man in the glass did the same.

Had his illness suddenly aged him, or how had the years caught up on him so quickly ? That line on his forehead came when Maggie got married, and he remembered someone laughing at a grey hair on his head at Teresa's wedding ; but this network of lines, this greyness, paling almost to white . . . Was he really old, or did he only look old ? How long was it since his mother died ? Ten years ? No, more. Fifteen ? Twenty ? More still. Good God ! his life was nearly over before it had begun, and he in whom every pulse raced in response to the corncrakes' call was mocked at by a girl for his white hair. It was shameful, unfair. He hated the farm, the place that had robbed him of his life, the sisters who had sucked him dry.

The next day he went to a lawyer in the town, and in a fortnight he had sold the farm for a trifling sum.

With the money in his pocket he went to Dublin, but he only stayed there a week, and then crossed to Liverpool, where he took a room in a frowsy hotel in a dusty street, and spent his money lavishly and stupidly on drink and women.

And there six months later he died. He who was a good farmer, and who should have been a husband and father, died in a stuffy city room in company with a blousy woman, who during his last ravings was running her hands through his trouser's pockets in search of loose cash, and as she did so these words came from the bed in the mutter of delirium : " The poor girls—look after them—look after them!"

April, 1914.

THE CHALICE

Mr. Appelby had hardly said the last word of the prayer for the church militant here on earth when the congregation scrambled to its feet and clattered down the aisle. Long ago this haste to have finished with the service used to pain him, but thirty-five years' residence in Lisfinny parish had taught him that the attitude of the Irish Protestant of the farmer class is—in appearance, at least—curiously undevotional. The Christian qualities are there in abundance, but perhaps from shyness, perhaps as a protest against the more evident and picturesque religion of their Roman Catholic neighbours, the Protestantism of the Church of Ireland in country places is a very reserved religion. The Dissenters are almost as severe, and it is only during the periodical visits of " preachers " or itinerant and vagrant religionists that the emotional side of the Irish Protestant's religion is allowed to appear. Then there is no state too exaggerated to which he or she will not go, no ectasy too hysterical, no fervour too profound.

The one exception to Mr. Appelby's undemonstrative congregation was a girl, delicate and consumptive, who Sunday after Sunday remained for the Communion Service. She waited, kneeling, her face covered by her thin white hands, while beside her sat her sister, solid, red, and certainly not demonstrative.

These two girls and one young man seated at the bottom of the church were the only members of the congregation who were waiting for the Communion Service. At first three people seemed to be very few, but after all, Mr. Appelby reflected, the congregation had not been large—twenty-five or thirty perhaps. Though the day was showery, there should have been more people, and as he put the vessels in order on the table (his fingers lingering unconsciously on the beautiful seventeenth-century chalice) he tried to recollect who should have been present ; but the names he remembered were of people too old or too feeble not to be excused, and the vague feeling of something slipping—slipping away from him which he had so often came back to him again, and it was only after a little effort of self-control that he was able to fix his mind on the service.

In the afternoon, after his dinner, sitting on the garden-seat beside his dahlias, he tried to analyse this vague feeling, tried to find a cause for this small congregation. The answer came quite rapidly and simply. The people were not there to come. What was slipping away was the people. They were not slipping away into the hands of the Roman Catholics or of the Methodists ; they were slipping away altogether, out of the country, out of life. The congregation of a hundred that he had looked down on every Sunday morning thirty years ago had dwindled—dwindled down to twenty-five. So many of the old had died and so many of the young had gone away, when the present generation passed on who would take their place ? He realised with a start that there was hardly anyone to step into their shoes. There were, to be sure, some young men and women among his congregation, but they were nearly all unmarried. He very rarely celebrated a marriage now. The district was poor and mountainous, money was scarce, and, somehow, the paucity of the people and the stagnation of life had given birth to a mad pride. Parents had sacrificed whole families to celibacy rather than contract inferior marriages for their sons and daughters. The lower did the family fortunes sink the more did blind pride point to a wealthy marriage as the only means of redemption. Mr. Appelby could recollect case after case when the want of a hundred pounds, or fifty pounds, or even less, had turned the scale between the creation of a new family or a houseful of fading daughters and the emigration of the young men. It was his everlasting regret that he was not wealthy, that out of his own pocket he could not smooth the way for some of these new marriages.

He had never felt this regret more poignantly than this afternoon, for all the three to whom he had administered the Sacrament were sufferers from this mercenary pride that was choking the countryside to death. The consumptive girl was the victim of the greed of a neighbouring farmer who had not considered her fortune worthy of his son, and so poor Kate Reardon grew thin and coughed while the young farmer in question went to America in a fit of temper, married in Chicago, and was at present managing to rear a family there in humbleness and comfort on

D

less money than his father considered he could live on at home. And now the tragedy was in danger of being repeated with Kate's sister—stout, simple Hannah—and the good-looking young man who sat at the bottom of the church. The parents on both sides made objections; Hannah hadn't enough money for Francey's father, and Hannah's father considered Francey's farm badly stocked.

Immersed in this tangle of unpleasant thoughts, the Rector looked up and saw Francey himself coming down the road. He called to him from the garden, and Francey crossed the stile.

" Good evening, Francey. I was just thinking about you and wondering whether you and the Reardons had come to any agreement."

" Why no, then, your Reverence. I was just over seeing the old man, and he doesn't seem inclined for it at all."

" And your father, too, is against the match ? "

" He is, then,"

" He thinks Hannah's fortune isn't. big enough ? "

" Yes, your Reverence."

" But he's nothing else against Hannah ?

I mean, if it wasn't for the money he'd be very pleased to have her for a daughter-in-law ? "

"Sure, what could he have against Hannah ? As I tell him, she'd bring more to the place than her fortune, for the country knows there isn't her like for butter and rearing turkeys."

" Yes, yes, Hannah's an excellent girl. But her father's against it too. . . . Well, well . . . do you think he's right in saying, Francey, that the farm is badly stocked ? "

" I do, to be sure, your Reverence ; but sure 'tis me father's own fault. He never spends a penny on it. Since the mother died he's got very close, as you know yourself. Sure, didn't he give you only ten shillings for the slating of the school-house. I declare to God I was ashamed to go to church to see the list on the door ; but Hannah's money would go to stocking the farm, and sure she'd wheedle more out of the old man ; a woman has a way of coming around a man, and in two or three years it would all be paid back—but sure, where's the use of talking, neither of them old men will agree to it."

" So it's only a few pounds stands between you and Hannah ? "

" That's all, but it's as wide as the sea ; wide enough, anyway, to send me out of this place."

" Would you go away, Francey ? "

" Well, I've a cousin in Australia who's doing well for himself, and why wouldn't I go out there ? "

" And what would become of your father and the farm ? "

" Yerra, let him pull along without me. Isn't it his own fault ? He has a right to give me a say in the matter ; if he doesn't, I'm not beholden to him. Good evening, your Reverence."

There was a harshness, almost a passion in the young man's words, and Mr. Appelby watched him climbing the stile with a pained feeling of dismay. He was so lithe and cleanly cut, so strong with his muscles, so nimble with his brain, such a fine type to become the father of a new generation. It seemed a thousand thousand pities that he and Hannah should be sacrificed for the want of a few pounds. Oh, if he had the money how quickly would he bring them together ! But he hadn't it ; there was no use dreaming. Francey would go to Australia, and Hannah would probably die an old maid. He shivered.

A shower was bringing the autumn afternoon to an end. As he walked up the path to the house the rain began to fall, and the wind scattered the dahlia petals on the path at his feet.

.   .   .   .   .

On Sunday afternoons before he had his tea it was Mr. Appelby's custom to wash and put away the Communion vessels, which he never kept in the church but in a locked box in his study. The paten and flagon were of commonplace modern silver, presented fifty years ago when the church was built ; but the chalice had come down from earlier times ; it bore the date 1603. It had a richly ornamented base, a graceful bowl, fragile now and worn in parts to an eggshell's thinness ; it was like a beautiful stately flower. Such things are not made now, but no one except the Rector knew of the existence of this beautiful thing in Lisfinny church. No record of the plate of the diocese had ever been made, and certainly not one of the bucolic lips that touched the bowl appreciated its beauty.

One man, indeed, had come to Lisfinny and raved of it, a lawless cousin of Mr. Appelby's who had once stayed at the

Rectory for two nights. He was an infidel and never went to church ; but he had seen the chalice in the Rector's hands as he gently polished it with the old linen cloth he kept specially for the purpose, and Mr. Appelby remembered well the scene that followed. The cousin, eager, extravagant, enraptured with its flowerlike beauty, had declared—for he was a connoisseur in all sorts of things—that it was priceless or, at any rate, worth its weight in gold. Of course, Henry, now that he knew its value, would sell it. It was too good to be wasted on Lisfinny, a successor unconscious of its beauty or its worth might replace it by something strong and modern, something more suited to Lisfinny and, by Jove ! he'd be right. It was all out of place in Lisfinny's gaunt, barren church. In an ancient Gothic cathedral, with choir boys and incense and all that sort of thing, it would be in its own atmosphere. He had a friend who would be crazy to buy it, who would give him anything he asked, almost ; and with the money Henry could put in the new heating apparatus the church needed so badly and supply all those things the church lacked. As to the morality of the proceeding, he would never bother about that end of it ; but his friend had bought many chalices from other clergymen —in fact, he specialised in ancient church plate : *they* had got over their scruples—and Henry might rest assured that everything would be done discreetly and liberally. The church's name was not on the chalice, only the name of the donor—a family long since extinct—and the date 1603. He'd give Henry his friend's address now ; he must write this very night.

And Henry Appelby had smiled and, without going into reasons—for how could he hope to convince this irreligious cousin ?—had steadily refused to accept the address or to do anything whatever in the matter, and had gently taken the chalice from his cousin's hands and locked it away in its box ; and when the cousin later on in a letter had sent him the address, Henry only wrote it down in his address book because he thought his sister might some day have to sell her old Irish teaspoons which he understood were of some value. That had all happened twelve years ago ; the cousin was dead, and the conversation had passed from his mind. So he thought, at least ; but this afternoon, holding the chalice in his hand, it all came back to him as vividly as if it had happened yesterday. It came back intertwined with Francey and Hannah and the dwindling congregation.

Most men when they grow old grow into bigoted old men, holding to their prejudices and opinions with a firmer grasp, binding the blinkers more tightly to their thoughts ; only a few men grow with age more uncertain in their opinions, more agnostic, more ready to reply " I do not know," to questions which in their younger days they would have answered with a vehement " yes " or " no." Henry Appelby was of this latter class. He often smiled at himself now when he recollected his religious and political bigotries of thirty years ago, when the parish priest had seemed his deadliest foe and Mr. Gladstone anti-Christ. Those bigotries had quite passed, but in addition to his religious and political tolerance there had come a broadening, a mellowing of his views as to what was ethically right and wrong. He grew more and more spiritually minded, and consequently less attentive to the letter of the law. Often he felt amazed and a little frightened at the laxity of his views about some matters. The Henry Appelby of 1880 would have judged and sternly condemned as unsound the opinions of the Henry Appelby of to-day on such subjects as the fourth commandment, divorce, and Home Rule. He was not a modernist, he did not read enough of current thought to class himself with any body of thinkers ; all he realised was (and he realised himself very little) that as he grew older he grew vaguer and more uncertain about most things. Even twelve years ago he had been able to dismiss his cousin's suggestion as utterly preposterous and unthinkable ; now he found himself considering and weighing it.

Considering and weighing, but holding himself off from any decision. Saying to himself, " Suppose I got a couple of hundred pounds for the chalice—and Oscar seemed to think I would—Francey could get married. I would get one of those electro-plated chalices— beastly things, but the quality of the wine will be the same. . . . But, of course, I have no right to sell it, it is not mine. . . . I hold the parish in trust ; its people are my people. I must hand on my trust to my successor ; he will receive less than I did, a congregation of twenty-five instead of a hundred. . . . It is a question of a dwindling congregation and a beautiful chalice and an increasing congregation and a modern chalice. . . . Some day there may be no congregation here at all.

What good will the chalice be then ? The church was made for man . . . of course, the Bishop wouldn't agree with me. . . ." And so on and so on for months, while the wet winter wrapped itself about Lisfinny and the question of Francey's marriage still hung unsettled.

But one day in early February, walking along the road that clung to the headland between the mountain and the sea, he was overtaken by the parish priest in his trap. He was a young priest new to the parish, and as soon as he had got Mr. Appelby beside him on the seat he broke out into a denunciation of the money-grabbing pride of Lisfinny, touching on the very subject so near Mr. Appelby's heart, the prevention of marriages. There was, Father Carroll declared, a young couple within a mile of where they were prevented from marrying for want of a dirty five-pound note. It was ruining the country. In any other country except Catholic Ireland it would have led to an outbreak of licence of the worse kind. Here it only led to the madhouse and America.

" Yes, yes, it's terrible," murmured poor old Mr. Appelby, and very much troubled, he walked up the avenue to the rectory. In the study he found a visitor waiting for him. It was Kate Reardon. 'In a few words she made her request; it was that the Rector would go and see her father and make him agree to her sister's marriage.

" If you don't, your Reverence, Francey will be off to Australia before the month is out, and Hannah—God help her—will be left behind to wear her heart out. She's not as strong as she looks, and she's fallen off in a fright these last months, as you can see for yourself, your Reverence. She got a weakness last market day after coming back from Lisfinny. Speak up to me father, your Reverence, you're too quiet (meaning no offence). There isn't a deal between him and Francey's father. If each side would halve the difference, I believe they'd come to a settlement."

`Her words following on Father Carroll's and always enforced by the shadow of her sister's fate, stirred the Rector to sudden activity. Before the night fell he had the two fathers facing each other in his study, and there, with a sturdiness which surprised himself as much as it did them, an eloquence and occasionally a harshness of tongue, he harangued and entreated them. Finally, it was beaten down to this : Francey's father was to spend fifty pounds on stocking the farm, provided Hannah brought three calves in addition to her fortune. The Rector promised to advance thirty of the fifty pounds, and one of the calves was to come from the rectory lawn. The banns were to be called the next Sunday.

When they had left him he sat down before his fire feeling suddenly very old and worn out after the struggle. He had committed himself now beyond any recall, and he knew the chalice would have to go. He took it out of its box and held it in his hands before the flickering firelight ; it had never seemed so flower-like in its beauty.

There is no need to relate the details of the weeks that followed : the negotiations for the sale, the forced secrecy—so hateful to Mr. Appelby's soul—the purchase of the ugly substitute. There was an agonising Sunday when for the first time he used the latter. When his own lips touched it he thought no one who had drunk from the old chalice could fail to notice the difference, and as he held it out to Kate Reardon he saw in a fraction of a second her start of wonder, her suspicion, her denunciation. But that was only imagination, and she handed it back to him evidently unconscious of any difference.

But there came another day not agonising. It was February again, and already in that mild southern county primroses were gleaming in the hedges and the hillside was flecked with furze blossom. Again the priest overtook him on the road and offered him a lift, but Mr. Appelby refused it. He was only going up the bohereen to the farmhouse on the hill.

" To be sure," said Father Carroll, " you'll be wanting to christen Francey's young son."

" Well, not to-day," said Mr. Appelby; " but I haven't seen the baby yet."

" Upon my word, Mr. Appelby, it was the best day's work you ever did when you made that match. And there's the Mulcahys below that you gave me the five-pound note for. Faith, Jim Mulcahy is running Francey very close, for if there's not a christening, there this month I'll resign my parish. Isn't it a fine thing now to see young families settling in the country ? "

" It is indeed."

" And, please God, they won't be the last."

" They won't," Mr. Appelby replied de-
cisively, thinking of the balance he still had
in the bank and the projected marriage he was
working for.

Months ago the question as to whether he
had done right or wrong had been settled for
ever in his mind ; but if it had not been,
certainly the sight of the little happy family
in the farm on the hill would have convinced
him.   Though Hannah was dark, Francey
was very fair, and the baby had taken after
him.   Its head was covered with a mist of
delicate pale hair, like old silver, Mr.
Appelby thought, like the chalice.   And was
it exaggerated and super-fanciful to think that
the baby took on something of the beauty
and the attributes of the chalice to which it
owed its very existence ?   Mr. Appelby
thought not, and as he knelt by the cradle—
the sunlight through the open door touching
his silvery hair and the baby's—he saw in it
the forerunner of a whole generation of
beautiful silvery children crowding the gaunt
church to the very door.

July, 1914.

A PAIR OF MUDDY SHOES

I AM going to try to write it down quite simply, just as it happened. I shall try not to exaggerate anything.

I am twenty-two years old, my parents are dead, I have no brothers or sisters ; the only near relation I have is Aunt Margaret, my father's sister. She is unmarried and lives alone in a little house in the country in the west of county Cork. She is kind to me and I often spend my holidays with her, for I am poor and have few friends.

I am a school-teacher—that is to say, I teach drawing and singing. I am a visiting teacher at two or three schools in Dublin. I make a fair income, enough for a single woman to live comfortably on, but father left debts behind him, and until these are paid off I have to live very simply. I suppose I ought to eat more and eat better food. People sometimes think I am nervous and highly strung : I look rather fragile and delicate, but really I am not. I have slender hands, with pale, tapering fingers—the sort of hands people call " artistic."

I hoped very much that my aunt would invite me to spend Christmas with her. I happened to have very little money ; I had paid off a big debt of poor father's, and that left me very short, and I felt rather weak and ill. I didn't quite know how I'd get through the holidays unless I went down to my aunt's. However, ten days before Christmas the invitation came. You may be sure I accepted it gratefully, and when my last school broke up on the 20th I packed my trunk, gathered up the old sentimental songs Aunt Margaret likes best, and set off for Rosspatrick.

It rains a great deal in West Cork in the winter : it was raining when Aunt Margaret met me at the station. " It's been a terrible month, Peggy," she said, as she turned the pony's head into the long road that runs for four muddy miles from the station to Rosspatrick. " I think it's rained every day for the last six weeks. And the storms ! We lost a chimney two days ago : it came through the roof, and let the rain into the ceiling of the spare bedroom. I've had to make you up a bed in the lumber-room till Jeremiah Driscoll can be got to mend the roof."

I assured her that any place would do me ;
all I wanted was her society and a quiet time.

"I can guarantee you those," she said.
"Indeed, you look tired out : you look as if
you were just after a bad illness or just before
one. That teaching is killing you."

The lumber room was really very comfortable. It was a large room with two big
windows ; it was on the ground floor, and
Aunt Margaret had never used it as a bedroom
because people are often afraid of sleeping on
the ground floor.

We stayed up very late talking over the
fire. Aunt Margaret came with me to my bedroom ; she stayed there for a long time,
fussing about the room, hoping I'd be comfortable, pulling about the furniture, looking
at the bedclothes.

At last I began to laugh at her. "Why
shouldn't I be comfortable ? Think of my
horrid little bedroom in Brunswick Street !
What's wrong with this room ? "

"Nothing—oh, nothing," she said rather
hurriedly, and kissed me and left me.

I slept very well. I never opened my eyes
till the maid called me, and then after she had
left me I dozed off again. I had a ridiculous
dream. I dreamed I was interviewing a rich

old lady : she offered me a thousand a year and comfortable rooms to live in. My only duty was to keep her clothes from moths ; she had quantities of beautiful , costly clothes, and she seemed to have a terror of them being eaten by moths. I accepted her offer at once. I remember saying to her gaily, " The work will be no trouble to me, I like killing moths."

It was strange I should say that, because I really don't like killing moths—I hate killing anything. But my dream was easily explained, for when I woke a second later (as it seemed), I was holding a dead moth between my finger and thumb. It disgusted me just a little bit—that dead moth pressed between my fingers, but I dropped it quickly, jumped up, and dressed myself.

Aunt Margaret was in the dining-room, and full of profuse and anxious inquiries about the night I had spent. I soon relieved her anxieties, and we laughed together over my dream and the new position I was going to fill. It was very wet all day and I didn't stir out of the house. I sang a great many songs, I began a pencil-drawing of my aunt—a thing I had been meaning to make for years— but I didn't feel well, I felt headachy and nervous—just from being in the house all day,

I suppose. I felt the greatest disclination to go to bed. I felt afraid, I don't know of what.

Of course I didn't say a word of this to Aunt Margaret.

That night the moment I fell asleep I began to dream. I thought I was looking down at myself from a great height. I saw myself in my nightdress crouching in a corner of the bedroom. I remember wondering why I was crouching there, and I came nearer and looked at myself again, and then I saw that it was not myself that crouched there—it was a large white cat, it was watching a mouse-hole. I was relieved and I turned away. As I did so I heard the cat spring. I started round. It had a mouse between its paws, and it looked up at me, growling as a cat does. Its face was like a woman's face—was like my face. Probably that doesn't sound at all horrible to you, but it happens that I have a deadly fear of mice. The idea of holding one between my hands, of putting my mouth to one, of—oh, I can't bear even to write it.

I think I woke screaming. I know when I came to myself I had jumped out of bed and was standing on the floor. I lit the candle and searched the room. In one corner were some boxes and trunks ; there might have been a mouse-hole behind them, but I hadn't the courage to pull them out and look. I kept my candle lighted and stayed awake all night.

The next day was fine and frosty. I went for a long walk in the morning and for another in the afternoon. When bedtime came I was very tired and sleepy. I went to sleep at once and slept dreamlessly all night.

It was the next day that I noticed my hands getting queer. " Queer " perhaps isn't the right word, for, of course, cold does roughen and coarsen the skin, and the weather was frosty enough to account for that. But it wasn't only that the skin was rough, the whole hand looked larger, stronger, not like my own hand. How ridiculous this sounds, but the whole story is ridiculous.

I remember once, when I was a child at school, putting on another girl's boots by mistake one day. I had to go about till evening in them, and I was perfectly miserable. I could not stop myself from looking at my feet, and they seemed to me to be the feet of another person. That sickened me, I don't know why. I felt a little like that now when I looked at my hands. Aunt Margaret noticed how rough and swollen they were, and she gave me cold cream, which I rubbed on them before I went to bed.

I lay awake for a long time. I was thinking of my hands. I didn't seem to be able not to think of them. They seemed to grow bigger and bigger in the darkness; they seemed monstrous hands, the hands of some horrible ape, they seemed to fill the whole room. Of course if I had struck a match and lit the candle I'd have calmed myself in a minute, but, frankly, I hadn't the courage. When I touched one hand with the other it seemed rough and hairy, like a man's.

At last I fell asleep. I dreamed that I got out of bed and opened the window. For several minutes I stood looking out. It was bright moonlight and bitterly cold. I felt a great desire to go for a walk. I dreamed that I dressed myself quickly, put on my slippers, and stepped out of the window. The frosty grass crunched under my feet. I walked, it seemed for miles, along a road I never remember being on before. It led up-hill; I met no one as I walked.

Presently I reached the crest of the hill, and beside the road, in the middle of a bare field, stood a large house. It was a gaunt, three-storied building, there was an air of decay about it. Maybe it had once been a gentleman's place, and was now occupied by a herd. There are many places like that in Ireland. In a window of the highest story there was a light. I decided I would go to the house and ask the way home. A gate closed the grass-grown avenue from the road ; it was fastened and I could not open it, ro I climbed it. It was a high gate but I climbed it easily, and I remember thinking in my dream, " If this wasn't a dream I could never climb it so casily."

I knocked at the door, and after I had knocked again the window of the room in which the light shone was opened, and a voice said, " Who's there ? What do you want ? "

It came from a middle-aged woman with a pale face and dirty strands of grey hair hanging about her shoulders.

I said, " Come down and speak to me ; I want to know the way back to Rosspatrick."

I had to speak two or three times to her, but at last she came down and opened the door mistrustfully. She only opened it a few inches and barred my way. I asked her the road home, and she gave me directions in a nervous, startled way.

Then I dreamed that I said, " Let me in to warm myself."

" It's late ; you should be going home."

But I laughed, and suddenly pushed at the door with my foot and slipped past her.

I remember she said, " My God," in a helpless, terrified way. It was strange that she should be frightened, and I, a young girl all alone in a strange house with a strange woman, miles from any one I knew, should not be frightened at all. As I sat warming myself by the fire while she boiled the kettle (for I had asked for tea), and watching her timid, terrified movements, the queerness of the position struck me, and I said, laughing, " You seem afraid of me."

" Not at all, miss," she replied, in a voice which almost trembled.

" You needn't be, there's not the least occasion for it," I said, and I laid my hand on her arm.

She looked down at it as it lay there, and said again, " Oh, my God," and staggered back against the range.

And so for half a minute we remained. Her eyes were fixed on my hand which lay on my lap ; it seemed she could never take them off it.

" What is it ? " I said.

" You've the face of a girl," she whispered,
" and—God help me—the hands of a man."

I looked down at my hands. They were
large, strong and sinewy, covered with coarse
red hairs. Strange to say they no longer
disgusted me : I was proud of them—proud
of their strength, the power that lay in them.

" Why should they make you afraid,"
I asked. " They are fine hands. Strong
hands."

But she only went on staring at them in a
hopeless, frozen way.

" Have you ever seen such strong hands
before ? " I smiled at her.

" They're—they're Ned's hands," she said
at last, speaking in a whisper.

She put her own hand to her throat as if
she were choking, and the fastening of her
blouse gave way. It fell open. She had a
long throat ; it was moving as if she were
finding it difficult to swallow. I wondered
whether my hands would go round it.

Suddenly I knew they would, and I knew
why my hands were large and sinewy, I knew
why power had been given to them. I got up
and caught her by the throat. She struggled
so feebly ; slipped down, striking her head

against the range; slipped down on to the red-tiled floor and lay quite still, but her throat still moved under my hand and I never loosened my grasp.

And presently, kneeling over her, I lifted her head and bumped it gently against the flags of the floor. I did this again and again; lifting it higher, and striking it harder and harder, until it was crushed in like an egg, and she lay still. She was choked and dead.

And I left her lying there and ran from the house, and as I stepped on to the road I felt rain in my face. The thaw had come.

When I woke it was morning. Little by little my dream came back and filled me with horror. I looked at my hands. They were so tender and pale and feeble. I lifted them to my mouth and kissed them.

But when Mary called me half an hour later she broke into a long, excited story of a woman who had been murdered the night before, how the postman had found the door open and the dead body. " And sure, miss, it was here she used to live long ago; she was near murdered once, by her husband, in this very room; he tried to choke her, she was half killed—that's why the mistress made it a lumber-room. They put him in the asylum afterwards ; a month ago he died there I heard."

My mother was Scotch, and claimed she had the gift of prevision. It was evident she had bequeathed it to me. I was enormously excited. I sat up in bed and told Mary my dream.

She was not very interested, people seldom are in other people's dreams. Besides, she wanted, I suppose, to tell her news to Aunt Margaret. She hurried away. I lay in bed and thought it all over. I almost laughed, it was so strange and fantastic.

But when I got out of bed I stumbled over something. It was a little muddy shoe. At first I hardly recognised it, then I saw it was one of a pair of evening shoes I had ; the other shoe lay near it. They were a pretty little pair of dark blue satin shoes, they were a present to me from a girl I loved very much, she had given them to me only a week ago.

Last night they had been so fresh and new and smart. Now they were scratched, the satin cut, and they were covered with mud. Some one had walked miles in them.

And I remembered in my dream how I had searched for my shoes and put them on.

Sitting on the bed, feeling suddenly sick

and dizzy, holding the muddy shoes in my
hand, I had in a blinding instant a vision of
a red-haired man who lay in this room night
after night for years, hating a sleeping white-
faced woman who lay beside him, longing for
strength and courage to choke her. I saw him
come back, years afterwards—freed by death
—to this room; saw him seize on a feeble
girl too weak to resist him; saw him try her,
strengthen her hands, and at last—through
her—accomplish his unfinished deed . . .
The vision passed all in a flash as it had come.
I pulled myself together. " That is nonsense,
impossible," I told myself. " The murderer
will be found before evening."

But in my hand I still held the muddy shoes.
I seem to be holding them ever since.

1917.

THE SPONGE

He hadn't been a week in Kyle when it came
to him suddenly, all in a flash, the theme he
had been waiting for. He knew it was somewhere of course all the time, just round the
corner, or rather *they* were there, for surely
their name was legion ; but how to overtake,
surprise, spring upon, seize and carry off even
one of the band was the problem that had
bothered him for the last fifteen years. He
was thirty-five years old now, and it was when
he was in the very early twenties that others—
friends and editors of magazines—began to
uphold his own conviction as to his power of
writing, his power even of winning by his
pen fame and success beyond the ordinary ;
the editors gave positive proof of their belief
in him by printing his stories and paying for
them, the friends talked largely and loudly
about him, and by the time he was twenty-five
he belonged to the select band of young
writers who " counted " and who could be

depended on to count for very much more in the future ; he had " arrived " very lightly equipped, on the strength of a few brilliant trifles, but heavy and interesting luggage was following him you felt sure ; when he started to unpack this, you might be assured of a display of riches dazzling to his generation.

What he had displayed to the public so far had been nothing of larger bulk than a number —a considerable number—of short tales. His genius (it was the word his friends used) had expressed itself in short stories of an unviolent kind. He could capture and put on paper in extremely lucid language most delicate and intricate psychic relationships, adventures of the mind, spiritual crises of the most subtle, fragile kind, making them so right, so true, that the most fastidious critics could not but praise them, and making them at the same time so simple and so exciting that ordinary people found pleasure in their perusal. He was never crude, and he was never precious.

But, of course, the short story was not going for ever to content him. They were mere trials of his wings, exhibitions of what he could do, wonderful feats, spectacular tricks undertaken to prove to himself how perfectly he was master of his machine, how even at his most daring moments his hands never hesitated or fumbled on the levers, never for an instant did he lose control. He was as capable he knew of long flights as of these brilliant brief dartings, of sustained soaring as of vivid flashings but—whither should he fly ? His flight would be so just and true, so brilliant and tremendous that it called for a worthy objective. He needed a great theme.

Many of the themes of his short tales were great, but in a tiny way. They didn't ask for sustained elaboration, they could adequately be dealt with and dismissed without going outside the limits which editors set to the " short story," he hadn't to compress them, they asked for no more space, demanded no large expanse of canvas. But he knew that there were themes that did demand space; his fellow-writers seemed to find them without great difficulty, why in Heaven's name couldn't he ?

And now after fifteen years of conscious searching he had found one. Found it in a flash of a second in Kyle Church, found it while he imagined he was following with attention the reading of the Second Lesson.

It was the parson who had supplied it ; little red-faced sleepy man, *he* was the theme, his sleepiness, his slovenly middle-age, his crumpled surplice, his stumbles over the prayers, his lack of attention. He had presented himself and all his appendages in a flash to Luke, had said to him in that clear unmistakable voice in which ideas always spoke, " Here I am, use me," and in the next second had made it clear that he couldn't be treated in a short story, that he possessed richnesses, amplitudes that asked for space unlimited to spread themselves upon, he presented himself as the theme for a novel.

The more Luke thought it over, the more rich, the more ample it became. It was vast. He saw that it wasn't going to concern itself only with the parson's personal history, it would imply the history of his whole class (which also was Luke's class), it would imply a certain amount of the history of Ireland. It started by presenting itself as the adventure of a clergyman who is young and energetic, who has led an active life in busy town curacies, and who is rewarded at an early age by being made rector of a country parish. His congregation would consist of twenty-five souls (Luke had counted twelve people in the country church); he would not have more than a day's work to do in the week, and gradually, slowly (how fascinating to watch in detail the slow advance !) he must lose all his fine freshness, all his enthusiasm, the spring of his activity must weaken, weaken, till he ended by becoming like sloppy Mr. —— whatever - his - name - was droning out the prayers. Should it be a study in negations, a tragedy in which the villain of the piece is just that nothing ever happens ? That idea dismissed itself; to make his tragedy worth the writing his hero must be rather exceptionally gifted for the act of living, and if so gifted he would be strong enough to break away from mere negation. No, his hero who loved life and people and activity, who belonged to the Church militant rather than to the church contemplative, must need for his undoing a train of events not necessarily far-fetched or violent, but a little out of the ordinary. Luke saw him not always patient, saw him unhappy. He decided that he must love and be unhappy in his love, he must love hopelessly, love, perhaps a Catholic—yes, by Jove that was it and——

The theme suddenly unfolded itself in quite unexpected amplitude. His hero became almost unimportant personally because so portentously important as an actor in a vast drama. The theme revealed itself in its true colours, wasn't ashamed of being labelled, boldly announced itself as being a study of the deathless antagonism between the two faiths.

But it wasn't going to be a violent drama. It must be for the most part unconscious, just the inevitable wearing down and away of the weaker of the two antagonists. It must never degenerate into being a " problem " novel, it must teach nothing, prove nothing, point out no reform that should be made. The big issue must be vast and impersonal, but all the detail of it immensely personal—the mere anecdote of it material that in other hands would go to make a " best seller."

At this point his theme seemed to him to lose its balance, its rightness and sanity became obscured. He turned his mind back to the starting-point, to the little slack, sleepy parson. But why sleepy and slack ? He didn't look like a man who had suffered actively, one couldn't suspect him of a tragic love affair ; in his case it must be a question of mere negation plus something, plus some force, some hidden power, that is to say *apparent* negation, something very active that ambuscaded itself behind a barricade of quiescence, something very powerful that pretended to be the personification of ineffectiveness, but what was it ?

His eyes searched the landscape, and the fields and woods, the damp sunshine and the soft wind smiled back at him in answer. He met them with a surprised incredulous " You ? " and they sighed a faint assent. His theme immediately righted itself : no wonder it had seemed out of balance, for, of course, the church was only half the theme, the other half was the country—this sunny friendly southern country which must smile in gentle welcome on his hero and gradually lap him round and fold him in and put him to sleep. He must be strong enough to fight the powers of darkness, but not the powers that came veiled in soft sunshine ; he mustn't be strong enough to fight the long mild wet winters, the enervating persistent south-west wind, the " stuffiness " of the valleys, the airless woods. These must weave around him thin webs, filmy threads so fragile as to be imperceptible in the spinning, they must gently blind his eyes to all distant views, softly seal his ears to all outside voices. In the end he must be offered a road of escape and must be too sapped of energy to take it, he must throw up the sponge with hardly a murmur, hardly a conscious gesture.

That was his theme in four words—throwing up the sponge. Hadn't Luke's class been doing it these three generations past, sometimes with groans and curses and struggles, sometimes with mute acceptance of the inevitable ? Wasn't his religion doing it, retiring without disorder, fighting a gallant losing battle ? It was part of the battle of class and creed not to admit that you were beaten, but the moment was quickly arriving when that attitude would become ridiculous, when the most dignified prayer was a *Nunc dimittis.* Now Luke should speak for his class finally and for ever, should throw up their sponge with a superb gesture, throw it up—as he exuberantly expressed it—with unerring aim, right into the blue, for all the world to wonder at. By Jove, what a theme, what a theme !

The small property he had unexpectedly inherited at Kyle included a pleasant little house, and by letting the land for grazing he found himself in possession of a sufficient income to live on. Eventually he would sell the property, but he determined to sacrifice three years to his theme. It only existed at present in broad outline, all the delicate intimate details needed careful filling in and a town-bred cosmopolitan like himself had no stock of knowledge to draw upon, he would have to collect it on the spot. But it was worth the trouble, it was worth three years of his life, it was worth, if necessary, five years.

During those years the details presented themselves quickly and in abundance. A chance acquaintance, a statement by a neighbour about someone else enabled him to create his Catholic family with ease. They were to be rich, would be the " big people " of his hero's parish, would be cultured and must offer to the young man all the beauties of art, music and literature which he would have missed—Luke felt he must have missed —during his curacies. Tennyson might have stayed at that Catholic house, it must at any rate have a tradition of literature and of music. Particularly of music, for Luke had never in his short stories had space enough to let himself " go " on this particular subject, but he promised himself now a veritable debauch. The family must be charming and gracious and must make the young man welcome till they found out the danger they and he were running. That danger must never culminate in anything approaching a "big scene" (Luke liked eschewing "big scenes"), it must be nipped in its earlier stages by someone, some more far-seeing relative, and the girl in question, quite unconscious of being the danger-spot, must be sent hurriedly away, must marry. Only when he found her gone must the poor hero realise that he loved her. And then there came into the scene, suggested, he knew not by whom, a man neither Catholic nor Protestant, a young squireen, but unlike other squireens, for he would hold himself aloof from his class, and though he would be a sportsman, a fisher, and a shooter, he would love beyond these pursuits music and the pleasures of a town. He would be a man with a twist in his nature or in his history—perhaps he would be illegitimate—would be lazy and without ambition, but with initiative enough to escape from the country a couple of times a year and to go to London, where he would spend his six months' savings in fast living, but a fastness that would include an orgy of concerts and operas. Luke's hero was to have a deep love of music, undeveloped until he came into contact with the Catholic family,

and then suddenly checked in its development
by the chill that would naturally fall between
the Rectory and the great house after the
girl's escape and marriage.. It is then that he
meets this man, and it was easy to appraise
the dangers that might arise from their contact.
His hero was friendless and alone, was disappointed in his love, was craving for music, for
life, for—for anything. He must be tempted
and must fall, must consent to a visit to
London with the squireen, a visit involving,
he knew, half-hinted-at sins, *saletés* of mind
and body. But something must intervene,
there must be no " crash," his friend must die
suddenly, violently, before the plan comes off,
and the poor hero must be left alone. That
was the essence of it, left alone. Left alone at
the mercy of the country, left alone to accumulate each year a thin layer of adipose tissue
which would numb and coarsen mind and
body. At the end a vigorous college friend
arrives, an overworked rector from Middlesex
or Lancashire, and offers him a road of escape,
offers him a curacy. He can't take it—or
does he take it and throw up the sponge in the
end, violently, by suicide?

That was the only detail in the story that
Luke hesitated over. Very soon the whole

train of events had learned their places, had learned to march in even file and steady step to his piping. Their march was so exact that no prelimimary drilling was necessary. Sometimes one of his short stories had demanded half a dozen preliminary essays before it could be induced to clarify itself, before it could be trained to march in rank. But his great achievement, his novel with the big theme needed no such tentative treatment, within eighteen months it stood four-square in his mind.

All except the very end. The exact alighting spot at the end of his long flight remained obscure. The exact method of the final chucking of the sponge.

He dreamed all day of his novel during that first hot summer he spent at Kyle ; he turned it over and over in his mind as he lay out in a long deck chair in front of the house among a tangle of weeds that had been once a flower garden. To retrieve that garden would be the work of a couple of years, and as he was so soon to sell the place the labour seemed hardly worth while. Had he intended to settle there permanently there were many improvements he might have made in house and grounds, but to spend money on what he was so soon to part from seemed foolishness.   In its own way it was a busy year for him, for if he cleared no gardens and mended no roofs he was all the while planning out and arranging the intricacies of his theme.   He dreamed of it during the long wet winter spent for the most part by the log fire in the shabby dining-room ; he talked of it to the literary friends who occasionally spent week-ends with him.

They all agreed it was good, it was big, and that he, and perhaps he alone, could do justice to it.   It was so good and big that it dwarfed everything else in his mind, its great spread of canvas demanded all his wind, there wasn't a puff left for the tiniest story.   His friends regretted this, thought that he might have spared a breath to propel some little craft, but he smilingly declared that impossible.   He was keeping back everything for his big effort.

Yet he hesitated before starting on the task of writing it.   It was all so nearly perfect, so arranged, it seemed a pity to begin until its perfection was absolute.   If he could only decide about the final chapter. Was it to be suicide or not suicide ?

" Write it, my dear fellow, to the penultimate chapter, and then, if you're still at sea, toss for it," his nearest friend urged him.

He couldn't do that. He felt all the rest to be so just, so true, that he couldn't descend to such base means. Besides he had no right to feel " at sea " about such an important point ; at times he half suspected his doubt must point to some fatal weakness in the construction of his book. He decided to wait, some day—to-morrow perhaps—the voice would be heard unmistakably saying " This is the way."

And he waited, the sponge in his hand Waited to give it that noble, heavenly spin, waited . . . waited. . . .

He grew to love Kyle, grew to love its river, the airless valleys, the leisurely life of the place. He stirred away from it less and less ; it seemed a pity to lose any of it when he was soon—next year probably—going to lose it completely and for ever.

And at last his patience was rewarded. As it was the parson who had given him the foundation-stone, so now it was the parson who supplied the final turret. He had come to see Luke, and, as he had often done before, the latter was delicately probing him, trying to find out what he felt and thought, or rather

how extensive was his absence of thought and
feeling. At last he asked him frankly why he
had spent thirty-five years in this parish,
why he had never tried to escape to some more
active sphere of work.

The parson as frankly answered him,
laughing good-humouredly.

"I suppose by the time I should have gone
I hadn't energy enough to go. There's something in this place, the climate——"

" Yes, yes," said Luke, and then suggested
that possibly in certain cases the loneliness
and absence of work, the objectlessness, the
" something " he spoke of might lead to
disaster or tragedy.

" Oh, it leads to drink sometimes—nothing
worse—and to that very seldom. One hasn't
energy enough to be wicked."

There it was in a flash ! Of course his
hero wouldn't have energy enough for suicide,
would be too wanting in initiative to destroy
himself. What an idiot he had been not to
see that obvious thing before ! But the
parson continued :

" Haven't you felt it too ? I mean the way
this place and climate take away one's
energy ? Why, when you came here you
said you were only coming for a couple of

years and were then going to sell the place. That's fifteen years ago—I was counting up yesterday—yet you're here still."

" Ah, I'm going now—to-morrow," Luke declared. " I've been waiting, looking for something, I've found it at last."

Yes, he'd go. He'd go back to a town and write his great novel in a year. He had it all now, every single detail of it from the first word to the last.

But, because it was so perfect, because he had it all " by heart," as children say, was it worth writing down ? He could write it well, he knew, no living writer could display it in all its details with his subtlety and simplicity. Other writers had more power and could have made of it a Zolaesque drama—he thanked God the idea had never come to *them* that *they* had never worshipped in Kyle Church !—and, of course many could have written it sentimentally ; but he, he only could treat the theme with balance and justice. His version would be so balanced and just that he wondered whether anyone would realise its absolute truth. No one would believe it, but that didn't trouble him, for the thing that mattered was that *he* believed it, he knew it to be true, it was his possession, bone of his bone and flesh of his flesh, the mere writing of it could not make it more completely his, and wasn't that all that mattered ?

And, if he wasn't going to write it, why leave Kyle ? Why not end his days there ? If he sold the place now it would be bought by some Catholic farmer, if he didn't sell it the cousin to whom he had willed it would be certain to do so, in either case their family, which had been connected with Kyle for more than two hundred years, would be gone, swamped, blotted out, the sponge would have been thrown up. What did he gain by going back to the world ? He would have to start to write again if he did so, and had he anything to say except this great thing which he no longer wanted to do more than whisper to himself ? Other writers had taken his place, well, let them keep it. But, possibly, he had grown a little sluggish, and he decided on a compromise. He gave himself another year in the country, after that he would go back to work.

   •   •   •   •   •

So he lives on at Kyle through the wet warm winters, the airless summers. He has grown stout. The weeds still grow in the garden, the slates are still missing from the roof. He is leaving the place next year, so why should he spend money on it ? He reads little, he thinks little. He is quite happy. When the moment comes for him to cease to exist his final gesture will be no defiant throwing of the sponge in the face of Heaven. Gently it will slip from his nervous fingers.

June, 1918.

THE WEIR

I.   A.D. 1800

"Don't leave me, Kate," said Florence
Desmond.

Kate had risen to leave the room but she
sat down again quickly. In her husband's
voice there was a harshness that demanded
instant obedience but along with that something tortured and anxious. She sat beside
the fire pretending to sew but stealing a look
every minute at the big man sitting loosely in
the armchair with his elbows on the dinner
table.

The meal was untouched. A mutton chop
had had a small piece cut of it, and pushed aside
had long ago grown cold ; a dish of potatoes
had not even been uncovered ; someone
had started to cut a slice of bread but the
knife still remained in the loaf. Florence
filled his glass from the decanter and rapidly
drank it.

“ Would you like me to get you some more ? ” Kate ventured.

“ No, thank you.”

“ I wish, my dear, you’d eat a little after your long ride.”

“ I’ve had enough.”

Kate sighed. Men were contrary creatures. A hundred questions were quivering on her lips but what use in putting them when Florence was in this mood ? Had he seen her sister, had she sent a letter, was she getting her the bonnet she had begged for ?— these questions were first in her mind but also she longed for all the gossip of the town. Goodness knows it wasn't every day her husband went to Dublin, and then to have him come back like this, with not a word for a dog . . . as if something had happened . . . as if . . .

“ Is the weir finished ? ”

“ It is indeed, Florence,” she said volubly, “ the last stone was put on it last week just before the rain came ; they had as many as twelve men working there. It looks very neat but, oh dear, I think it's spoiled the place. 'Tis very damp and vapourish now and the river so sluggish, I wish you’d never allowed it.”

" If I don't like it I can have it pulled down."

" Can you ? I thought there was an agreement between you and the Nashs, I thought——"

" I tell you I can take it down. 'Twould cost money, no doubt, but I have the power." He spoke violently as if to convince himself.

Silence fell until he rose and unlocked a cupboard and took out a bottle of brandy. He drank off a wine-glassful and filled the glass again. Kate watched him narrowly. Florence was not a drinking man.

The spirit loosened his tongue and he stood in front of the fire talking disjointedly.

" There's nothing certain . . . till a thing's done you don't know how it will look or what result 'twill have. They say ' This is good and that is bad,' but they don't *know*. . . . I acted for the best, but . . . I feel frightencd, I suppose I'm growing old . . . when I did it 'twas as if someone had laid a heavy hand on my shoulder, something that weighed me down . . . coming home I wished I could undo it all . . . but I acted for the best."

" But you said just now you could make the Nashs take down the weir."

" The weir ? Oh yes, *that* will be all right, but . . . " he sighed.

The door opened and his son came in, a tall man of thirty.

" Good evening, James," said Florence.

His greeting was not returned. For half a minute he stood looking at his father. He seemed to be trying to control himself, trying to find unviolent words.

" So you voted for it after all."

His father nodded. " I did."

" When you left here you were against it."

" I changed my mind, I acted for the best."

" What made you change ? Who made you change ? "

" I thought things over."

James laughed in a strangled way.

" Thought things over ! How much did they give you ? "

Florence did not understand. " What ? "

" I say, how much did they give you ? How many thousands ? Or did they make you a lord, or are you a placeman ? What was your price ? "

Kate breathed a frightened protest. Florence drew himself up with dignity.

" You forget yourself, James."

G

" You couldn't even make a bargain, you've sold us for nothing at all ! "

" When you're cooler you'll—regret those words, James. I'll forgive them. There was no bargain, there was no question of buying or selling. I voted for the Union because I believe it will be the best thing for Ireland."

" You left here believing the other thing."

" I did what I thought was right. It's done now. There is no use in fighting against it."

The young man laughed.

" Oh, there is plenty of use ! You're mistaken if you think we're going to take this quietly. We've right on our side, the right of the law, the right of God. We'll break the Union."

" Don't be foolish, don't waste your time. You cannot——"

" I will, and it won't be waste of time. I'd give ten years of my life to undo this. Ten years ?—I'll give twenty if it's necessary but it won't be. You'll be travelling up to Dublin again to take your seat in Parliament before ten years have passed."

.   .   .   .   .

James was wrong. He himself died forty years later. The Union still held.

II.   A.D. 1860

Approaching the weir the fall of the ground was very slight and even before it was built the river there had flowed sluggishly. Now it had lost all appearance of movement and for three-quarters of a mile above the weir the river formed one long, deep pool. Weeds clung to the gravel and grew longer and thicker year by year; they floated on the surface in a green, slimy mass, and one kind broke into white, starry, sickly-sweet flowers in May. Towards the bank water-lilies grew, and a plant with dark, heart-shaped leaves. The bottom of the river became muddy; dark trout swam lazily between the lily stems; it was almost impossible to tempt them with fly or bait; in the summer the dragon-flies sunned themselves on the broad lily leaves.

In wet weather the river overflowed its banks and even at other times the fields by the river had a certain soddiness. Rank weeds throve, the yellow iris spread and the grass grew in coarse turfs so that the cattle hardly cared to eat it. On summer evenings the shallow valley was filled with a white fog which curled along the sides of the low hills, in winter the trees dripped with moisture.

The house stood a little above the river, separated from it by a small wood. It stood not high enough, or far enough away, to escape the cold fogs, which killed the tender plants in the garden and forced the hardy plants into an exuberance of coarse foliage. Even through the summer they had to keep fires burning in the sitting-rooms.

Where the wood fringed the river the trees died. The water soaked their roots and they died slowly, the branches rotted and cracked and dropped, a tree would be ten years a-dying and the fungus grew from every crumbling stump.

Facing the river at the edge of the wood, under a tree, was a rustic seat, and on it, one September afternoon in the year 1860, sat Florence Desmond, son of James Desmond who had set out to break the Union. Though the sun was shining he wore a heavy coat and across his knees lay a plaid shawl. His son, a boy of fifteen, was sitting beside him.

" I blame my grandfather," he was saying, " he shouldn't have allowed the Nashs to build the weir. It's done them no good and it's done us no good."

" Knock it down," said the boy.

" Easier said than done, Jim. We have a certain right over it, but it's all a lawyer's tangle, it's hard to find out what's what. My father tried, I tried. Nothing happened except lawyers' bills."

" I hate it, it's rotting everything. The paper peels off the rooms in the house, the moss grows in the gravel."

His father coughed painfully.

" I know. And it's killing me. I'm only fifty-five and I'm dying."

The boy's eyes suddenly were pricked with tears. To hide them he started up.

" I'll knock it down, I will, I will. If it takes every penny of my money and every year of my life."

" No, no. Come here, Jim. Listen. Forget it all. Forget the weir, forget Ireland. You'll wear your life out for nothing as I did and my father before me. Forty years he gave to it. Think of it, Jim, forty years ! And nothing to show for it all except maybe Emancipation. And I've given all my years and I've less to show. I was like you once, Jim, I was young, I was clever, I might have done things but they've killed me for nothing; this endless struggle, year after year, and then this place, the dampness, the deadness . . . we've given two generations. Two's enough, Jim, you must go away, there are openings in America for the Irish, forget this place. Promise me you'll go, promise. . . . "

" I'll smash the weir and go."

" No, before, before . . . " the dying man pleaded, his body shaken by a cough.

III.   A.D. 1891

Jim meant to go, for two years after his father's death he meant to go, and then he gradually became convinced that to do so was to play the coward. His father and grandfather had made their mark in Irish politics, there was a future there for their descendant, there was a duty there, a mission. The States, too, offered a future, Philadelphian cousins wanted him to join them, they had a flourishing business, they would help him, in ten years he could be a rich man. But all the reasons for going west seemed to him selfish ones and, with hardly a regret, he finally decided not to leave Ireland. He was a brilliant boy, a lovable boy, fragile—for he inherited something of his father's delicacy—

and impressionable. He had sudden enthusi-
asms and equally sudden depressions, a gift
for friendship, unswerving loyalty, unselfish-
ness so pronounced as to be almost absurd.

He had not only a brilliance of manner,
he had also a brilliance of brain. The
Desmonds had never been bookish people,
but he took some queer twist and might.have
become a scholar. The college would have
liked to have kept him with them, they urged
him not to throw away his talents, tried to
dazzle him with talk of prizes, fame, honour.
But he shut his eyes to them as he had shut
his eyes to the States.

He threw all his gifts at his country's feet.
He gave her his youth, his talents, his money,
his years, he spent himself prodigally and
asked for nothing in return. Nothing, that
is to say, for himself—for Ireland he asked
everything.

He was too unselfish, too fine in mind and
character to win any great personal success in
politics. His name will never appear in
history ; even his own generation, to a large
extent, was unaware of him. He was .so
upright that he could be ignored.

He was among the first to recognise Parnell's
genius. For a time there came a sharp

struggle between his loyalty to others and the attraction of the new leader, but when the touchstone of Ireland's need had been applied there could be no dubious answer, and though he was one of the first to follow that cold, dark man, his old friends forgave him. The attraction he felt grew deeper, became affection, finally became worship. For the first time in his life he became a little blinded, his judgment grew unbalanced, his country had become flesh, became embodied in a man, underwent a mysterious incarnation. His dream walked a god amongst men.

He never imagined failure. Such a thing was an impossibility, a violation of the law of nature. There surely would be disappointments, delays, wearinesses, vexations of spirit innumerable, but the end was certain. Ten years or twenty years distant, it was coming inevitably.

Even when the crash came he didn't lose heart. It was a staggering blow but not a fatal one. His god was there, was living; it was only a question of time.

But his god was mortal flesh and sickened and died.

James Desmond walked beside the river trying to bring himself into adjustment with the new situation. He could not do so, he had been mastered too long by one idea. He hadn't sanity enough to thank God for what his hero had done, he could only remember what his hero had not been able to do.

And if Parnell couldn't do it who could ? Someone might arise in the future, having some different quality that might be necessary for success, but would he live to see it ? He was nearly fifty years old; could he live and watch for twenty years and perhaps be disappointed in the end ?

He leaned against a dying tree. Under it a rustic seat had stood once but long years ago it had rotted away. He thought of his father's dying words, he thought of his own wasted life. He, too, had a son, a boy of twelve ; was this waste to go on from generation to generation ?

Should he warn the boy as his father had warned him ? What use had it been in his own case, what use would it be in his son's ?

He felt old, tired in brain and body. How many thousands of miles, he wondered, had he travelled in life to undo his ancestor's work, how many thousands of pounds had he spent ? And what might he not have done with his life ? " ' We throw the sand against the wind,' " he murmured to himself, " no, not sand—time, gold, genius, youth, happiness." He was thinking not only of himself, all over the country the same awful sacrifice of brains and time and money was going on and would go on and must go on.

But not in his case, he was spent, worn out.

The mist rising from the river blotted out the landscape. It wrapped itself round him, he was alone in a damp, grey world. And the chill and terror of it laid cold fingers on his heart and he began to cry feebly like an old man who has lost everything.

    .   .   .   .   .

A week later Florence, his son, playing by the weir saw a dark mass slowly turning under the water and dim white fingers that seemed to claw feebly at the resisting wall. Without understanding what it was he cried out and ran, frightened, to the house. An hour later his father's body was dragged to the bank.

IV. A.D. 1916

After the rain it was pleasant to walk by the river in the warm April sunshine, it was pleasant to push the perambulator along the smooth path, it was pleasant to sit on a rustic seat under a tree. Rain had fallen heavily and persistently for three days and the two women—Mary Desmond and her husband's sister Kate—had been imprisoned in the house. Now on this sunny Tuesday morning they sunned themselves on the river bank, turning over a bundle of patterns of bright summer fabrics, stitching at little baby garments and getting up every minute to move the perambulator, now into the sun, now into the shade.

" How the sun brings out the colours," said Mary Desmond. " I think that pink is too bright now, I prefer the blue after all. Sun makes all the difference in the world. These last days have been dreadful, the rain got on my nerves, I was as cross as two sticks. Was I very horrid, Kate ? "

" At times you were rather horrid," Kate said, smiling, " but I made allowances for the weather. I'm more used to it, living all my life above this poisonous weir, but even I feel the effect of it at times."

" Florence really has hopes of getting it taken away."

" So had father, I believe, and his father before him."

" Well, I hope it will be gone soon. I shouldn't like Baby to grow up in this damp place. Poor chap, such a wet birthday and Florence away in Dublin. It was annoying, you know. . . . I wish he'd come back. . . . Do you like that greenish one ? "

" Not particularly. . . . You heard to-day ? "

" No, no letters came at all; it seems strange."

" He's sure to be back before the end of the week."

" Perhaps. . . . Kate, do you know what he's doing in Dublin ? "

She turned full on her sister-in-law as she spoke. Kate moved a little uneasily.

" How should I know ? "

" His last letter . . . so strange . . . so —I can't make it out."

" I didn't hear. What did he say ? "

Mary fumbled for the letter.

" Oh, it's in the pram . . . Here it is. . . . It's only this sentence. Listen. ' I'm awfully sorry not to be down for Baby's birthday. I can't help it and I can't explain why I'm stuck here. You'll know soon. Tell him I did what I thought right, that I trust he will think the same and act as I did, for I know this is not the end.' Really, Florence must be raving. How can I tell things like that to a kid who was only a year old yesterday? That was written on Sunday."

" It's very strange," Kate said. " I don't like it somehow."

" It frightens me. There's been—he's been keeping something from me lately . . . Kate, could you look after Baby if I went to Dublin ? "

" To Dublin ? "

" Yes, I feel something—something horrible is happening, it's as if something had come between us, he seems far away; I can't explain what I mean, but if I don't get a reassuring letter to-morrow morning I'll go up by the afternoon train."

   .   .   .   .   .

Just then in Dublin Florence's only thought was of the weir. He lay on the ground staring at it. First it had seemed like a brick wall but he knew now it was the weir. It was very strong, stronger than he had ever believed it to be, the great stones fitted closely one to another. He stretched his hand out and touched it.

As he moved there came a sudden rush of water. It passed over his head, engulfing him. It was foul, choking water with a sickening smell and bitter to taste. He struggled for his life and breath ; slimy weeds entangled his feet, dead, rotting things hampered him, dark, blind eels slipped slimily through his fingers ; with a tremendous effort he reached the surface spluttering.

"It must go," he said aloud. "From the beginning it's been wrong, it's poisoned things, it's done no good to anyone, stagnant water, rotting things rubbing against each other ; if the law won't take it away we must pull it down with our naked hands."

"Open his coat," said a voice.

"I was a fool to waste my time with anything else. It's the weir that matters. It's a canker, a poison bed. It's no good to the others. Can't they see, my God, can't they see ?"

"Cut his shirt."

"I'll pull it down, if it kills me I'll pull it down . . . the river will flow again . . . that's blood, the stones are sharp . . . they're loosening . . . I feel the water trickling through . . . water . . . years ago."

He was silent, pulling down the weir stone by stone. He tore at the stones with his hands, he shook them, he loosened them. One great stone was pressed to his side and the tighter he pressed it the more freely flowed the water. The stone had a sharp edge, the pain was terrible, almost beyond human endurance, but if he let it go the weir would build itself up again. He pressed it tighter, closer to his side, and the pain devoured him like a flame. But though it devoured him, the stone loosened and rocked in his hand and broke at last in a torrent of water. The weir faded ; pain faded.

" Take it outside," said a voice, " and, some-one, fetch a mop."

.   .   .   .   .

The sun went behind a cloud, the women shivered.

" Let's go back to the house," said Mary. " There's a—a sort of deadness here by the weir. . . . Look, Kate, he's asleep ! Isn't he the image of his father ? "

1918.

EDUCATION

HE was more tired than he cared to own. He had borne the journey to Dublin without conscious fatigue, had sat on deck talking to Mrs. Conder after dinner and till they reached Holyhead, but once stretched out in his sleeper fatigue had sprung on him like a beast unleashed, had gripped him in every muscle, making sleep an impossibility.

Particularly, of course, it had settled itself in his leg and back. There it was perfectly at home; it had lived there day and night for more years than it was pleasant to remember, and had learned long ago a thousand subtle ways of claiming possession of him. It had never been more subtle than at this moment, never more elusive, so that when he tried to bring relief to his knee by changing his attitude it immediately became obvious that the pain had all accumulated in his back, and when he turned his attention there it fled away, throwing spears of pain as it fled, to settle somewhere else.

But his brain was too busy and excited to bother to pursue it. After half an hour's tossing and turning he accepted the bodily fatigue with resignation as he had accepted it so often before, and accepted too the fact that something was unleashed in his brain, was galloping and racing. He gave it its head with a sigh and waited for what it would show him.

At first there came a succession of inconsequent objects which only he could piece together and make sense of. Foremost among them was a worn sofa, a grand piano and himself endlessly progressing from the sofa to the piano and back again. In the carpet which lay between his feet seemed to have worn a deep track during sixteen years, those sixteen years since that accident with the pony-carriage, which had broken and bruised him but which had bruised his mother more deplorably, more intangibly, in her brain, in her nerves, making it an agony for her to lose sight for one moment of her boy, her only child. His father was in no picture of his brain, yet always ominous in the background, not dead but swallowed up years ago in some financial disaster, something dishonest and disgraceful that had for ever tarnished his

H

reputation, and caused him to fly from Doon House, from Ireland, from the life of his wife and child. Gradually they had lived down the disgrace of that cowardly flight; it was difficult for anyone to deny sympathy to the pathetically nervous deserted wife, and more difficult to deny anything to the boy, so stricken in body, so sacrificed to his mother's broken nerves; impossible, finally, as the years went on to deny anything to his genius.

For it was not for nothing that the track had been worn between the sofa and the piano, not for nothing those hours of practice as long—and longer—than his strength would permit, not for nothing those weekly visits of a Professor, a real Doctor of Music, from the neighbouring town. At sixteen young Martin was precocious, and at twenty he played the Professor off the piano and out of Doon House.

Life went by to a lilt of music, each hour of it set to a gay or sad air. Wasn't the train at this moment beating out the first subject of that dearly-loved Chopin sonata? As he hummed it the rhythm altered and became a merciless, hurrying *motif* from the last movement of *Scheherazade*—extraordinary how the throb of the train fitted it, how it came

down with a strong accent, a " rat-tat-tat "
just where it was required. He wondered
whether Mrs. Conder was awake and listening
to it.

He owed her *Scheherazade* and Borodin and
many others whose names had been unknown
to him a month ago, as unknown as her name.
Tom Conder had taken the Castle for a
month's fishing and she came too to entertain
her husband's guests, Colonels and Majors and
Captains, a seemingly endless succession of
them, all so alike to her and all so dull, but
friends of dear old Tom's and for his sake
gladly welcomed. It was fisherman's weather
and she spent long wet days in the house
reading and practising her songs. Ten days
of .this found her bored, and when she was
approached and asked to sing at a local
concert in aid of some all-deserving charity
she gladly consented. But she must have an
accompanist, and the schoolmistress who was
recommended to her stared helplessly at the
most simple of her songs and rose from the
piano stool after ten minutes' labour, saying,
" You'll have to get Mr. Martin, he's the only
one here will be able to play that class of song.
You've a gorgeous voice only it's a pity you
couldn't sing something more simple-like—

more of an air to it—sure Doon won't know what to think of this. I'd like you to beat the Canon's niece, three encores she got the last time and such airs as she gives herself, though she hasn't much voice at all, only the way she sings, half play-acting all the time."

Mrs. Conder enquired further. It seemed that Mr. Martin, too, gave himself " airs " but in this case he was entitled to do so. He wouldn't play accompaniments for everyone, and wouldn't play " that cheap music." But he made people like what he played, it was " like a miracle " what he could do with a piano, especially with his own piano, which was a big one, not like the one at the school with two notes dumb and another that always stuck down and was a great bother till you learned the knack of lifting it with your thumb. She'd send Mr. Martin over to the castle at once; the sooner the programme was settled the better.

He came the next morning, driving over in a low pony-carriage. He walked, even in the house, with the help of a stick and was at first very shy, but as soon as he had limped over to the piano his shyness disappeared and they were soon deeply intent on the songs.

That morning came back to him now as the prelude to many other happy meetings. He had never before had a chance of playing with a good singer. He had played a good deal with a fiddle, but the bank clerk who played it so obviously preferred Braga's *Serenata* to a Mozart sonata (though he could play both) that their musical communion was limited. He had never before—not, at any rate, since the days of the Professor—met a musician so nearly his equal in taste. It was wonderful not to have to apologise for liking Brahms and Beethoven better than Braga, wonderful not to run the risk of being thought to have " airs."

But he had from the first, from the moment his Professor had left him, rather finely taken the risk of that. He would play anywhere and for anyone but only the music he himself liked. And his rather haughty attitude justified itself. At first Doon sat restless or bored, then it gave grudging admiration to his playing, it ended by becoming immensely proud of him. His young handsome face, his limp, his wonderful playing combined to make him a personage. No town in the county possessed any person that could touch him for allure. A doctor's daughter

who had been to school in Paris and who lost
her heart at once to his dark hair and his
white, magical fingers, called him "a great
artist." Doon laughed when it heard the
term but in a week it had adopted it and
whispered it at tea-parties and in drawing-
rooms over shops ; and the piano tuner was
kept busy after the awful occasion (Mrs.
O'Brien's evening party at the National
Bank) when Martin after playing a few bars
had begged to be excused until some future
occasion when his hostess's piano might be
less excruciatingly out of tune.

His final rehearsal with Mrs. Conder took
place at his own house, and after tea he played
to her for an hour and then sat with her over
the fire and talked to her in the dusk. He
told her his rather miserable story and asked
for her advice. His mother was dead now,
had died three months before, he was free at
last, he could travel.

" Certainly you must travel," Mrs. Conder
declared, " and you can't do better than begin
by travelling back with us to London. Come
with us when we go at the end of the month."

" What an idea ! "

" It's a good one. You'll be more comfortable with us than at an hotel. Manchester

Square is quite convenient. There is a little good music to be heard, some bad opera ; you shall go to everything you want to hear."

" Bad or good it's bound-to be better than Doon music. I hear nothing. but what I make myself. I haven't been to London since I was twelve; when mother's nerve went she couldn't travel and as I had always to be within call of her I couldn't travel either."

" Then travel now to Manchester Square."

" No, no, you're—you're grand people. I'd be out of the picture. Why, I haven't even a presentable suit of dress clothes ! "

" That doesn't matter nowadays,"

He refused the invitation, but it was re-newed several times during the weeks that followed, and Tom brought a good-natured pressure to bear on him. And now here he lay, bright and sleepless, travelling to London, with Tom snoring quite close to him and Mrs. Conder not far away. Travelling to London, to music, to life, with the wheels throbbing out that pitiless phrase from *Scheherazade.*

.   .   .   .   .

In the car from Euston as they travelled towards Manchester Square, looking at his pallor, she told him she didn't want to see him before dinner-time nor even then unless he felt inclined. But by tea-time he had had some sleep, and wandered downstairs and found her in the drawing-room. She had expected "nobody," she said; but six or eight people were talking and drinking tea, and to them he was introduced in a comprehensive way. Mrs. Conder labelled him—as she labelled everyone; his tag read "Mr. Martin who has come over from Ireland with us to hear music," and on these terms he got on with the strangers very well. Most of them seemed musical and gossiped about who was "back," and who was coming, and a new girl who was a marvel, and an old man who was impossible but such a dear. All this was out of Martin's depth, and he could only listen, brightly interested. The Blüthner lay temptingly near, and he longed to play. After his night of pain and his deep sleep he felt full of inspiration, and to these people he could have expressed himself without fear of being misunderstood.

He had come to London to listen, and it was only now that it suddenly flashed upon him that here at least and for the first time in his life he would find an audience. Not, of course, a Queen's Hall audience, not a concert with advertisements and tickets and a printed programme, but an audience now and then in this spacious room of chosen people, people like himself to whom music was a passion, who might differ from him, but who would understand him. Mrs. Conder would gather them there from time to time and he would play to them as he had often played to her; by pleasing her friends he would repay a little of all he owed her.

It was intoxicating this idea of at last finding an audience. At Doon everyone liked music, it was genteel to like music, but only one or two had really cared. The doctor's daughter was one of them but Martin had regretfully come to believe that the reasons why she " liked " so enthusiastically were not musical ones, that they had too much to do with the personality of the player. But here his personality would be a negligible quantity and he would be liked for his music alone.

There was nobody at dinner except a widowed sister of Mrs. Conder's, who was staying at Manchester Square. Tom had gone to the country to some friends, and would be away for a week. " Meanwhile," his wife declared, " .we'll have an orgy. Where is the paper, what is there we can hear ? "

Not so very much as it turned out. To-morrow an orchestral concert, old classical stuff. " Let me off that, I've a committee, but you must go, you shall have the car," the next day nothing, the day after De Burgh and his fiddle, two days later the great, the incomparable Dremling.

" You'll love him, he's enormous in size and in his art, he's a dear old-fashioned thing. He'll begin with a Scarlatti, then some Bach, then a big, big, Beethoven, a Chopin or two, some Brahms, and, to show he's quite up to date, he'll finish with something French and modern which he simply hasn't the remotest idea how to play. But we'll go away before he gets to that. Now play to me a little and then I'm going to send you to bed."

He played to her for an hour while she sat over the fire scribbling notes with great rapidity.

" You're in good form to-night," she told him. " No, I won't sing but I'm asking a few people in to-morrow night, a cousin of mine who sings and her husband who plays the violin and a young man—the only man in London who can play Debussy.'

"I hope he'll come," Martin said. "I'm like Dremling, I can't play that modern stuff. Will you sing those French songs I floundered so over; will he play with you?"

.   .   .   .   .

"Mr. Martin hasn't a word to say, Dremling has left him speechless. The dear man was in great form I admit. Play to us Hugo, please, Mr. Martin refuses to touch a note."

"Can you bear me after Dremling?" Hugo asked.

"I always like to hear you. You've no pretensions, you know you're not a pianist."

Martin lay on the sofa, his eyes closed. He said nothing. Mrs. Conder spurred Hugo on to one piece and then another until at midnight he got up to go.

Martin got up to bid him goodnight.

"You're not in good form to-night, I'm afraid," Hugo said kindly as they shook hands. "I want to hear you play, perhaps you will next time I come."

"I? Oh, I can't play the piano," the tired young man replied.

"You expect me to believe that?" Hugo laughed.

Mrs. Conder followed Hugo to the hall.

When she returned to the drawing-room,
Martin was standing in front of the fire, his
elbow on the mantelpiece, his back turned to
her.

"Go to bed," she said kindly, laying her
hand on his arm.

He turned round.

"Good gracious, how tired you look!" she
exclaimed.

"Why didn't you tell me?" he said.

"Tell you? . . . What?"

"That I'm no good, that I can't play."

"But you can play; you have given me a
great deal of pleasure."

"You're always so kind," he said bitterly.

"Kind?"

"Thank you, at any rate, and most sin-
cerely for not gratifying my conceit by asking
me to play to your friends here. The one
consolation I have is to remember that, however much I may have made a fool of myself
at Doon, no one but you has heard me play a
note here."

"But——"

"You were so kind, you kept on sparing
me—you always suggested I was tired. Thank
you, thank you a thousand times."

"Why? . . . What?"

" And I dreamed I'd find an audience here, an audience worthy of listening to me. Worthy of *me !* "

" Mr. Martin, why——"

" I can't play the piano," he said squarely.

" That's because you've just heard Dremling. He takes the conceit out of us all."

" Dremling ? Oh, it's not Dremling—he least of all ! What I've learned in four days ! The way you raised your eyebrows that afternoon I was so enthusiastic about the girl who accompanied you. " Oh ! she's not a pianist," you said. The woman who played the Brahms sonata with your cousin, the boy who played Debussy, the magic, the poetry of it, the things he made the piano do, the girl who played the Beethoven concerto at the concert, Dremling this afternoon, and then Hugo."

" Hugo ? "

" Hugo, worst of all."

" But Hugo can't play."

" That's it, that's it, he ' can't play '; you've said so yourself; and that girl who accompanied you ' can't play '; and that man who was at the piano for an hour yesterday afternoon ' can't play.' None of them can play, but they all play as well as I do— better."

" My dear man, you play much better than Hugo or Jerry."

" They don't pretend to be pianists—they never practise, they've not given their whole lives to it as I have. Why were you so kind to me at Doon ? Why didn't you tell me the truth ? Or did you think I wouldn't believe you, that it was better I should find out for myself in this dreadful way ? Was that why you brought me to London ? "

Poor Mrs. Conder turned away.

" My God, when I think of it I grow hot all over. Do they all know at Doon ? Is it a kind conspiracy because I'm unfortunate, crippled ? Are they sighing behind my back : ' Poor Mr. Martin, I suppose we must ask him to play. He thinks he can ' ? "

" I am sure they all think you play beautifully," she said gently.

" No, no, there'll be some who must see through me, someone like you, some stranger will come from time to time and listen and *know*. Oh, the things I've said, the attitude I've taken up ! "

He put his hands over his face.

" I can never go back there. I can never face Doon again."

" What nonsense."

“They’ll say ‘ like father like son ’; both
deceive, cheat, pretend, lie.”

“ You haven’t lied, you’ve said nothing
you didn’t believe to be true, done nothing
you didn’t believe.”

“ They’ll never believe that I didn’t know.
I’m losing the only thing I ever had or rather
finding out that I never had it at all.”

“ You have it.   Yes, it’s in you.   If you
had been well taught, if you had had a chance
of hearing music, if your mother had let you
travel.”

“ If, if, if,” he mocked.   “ If I had never
been born, if the pony had kicked my head in
in that time instead of only my back.”

“ You are cruel to yourself.”

“ I must pay myself out for all that secret
complacency, that feeling of superiority.   I
despised them, I felt I was a great man.”

“ You are great compared with them.”

“ How do you know ?   They’re so polite, *you*
were so polite.   You deceived me as entirely
as they did.   I can never play to them
again.”

“ You can go back and tell them what you
have learned here.”

“ They will pretend not to believe me, they
will half-persuade me, I’ll end by playing for

them but always with the feeling that there
may be one amongst them, like you, who
knows, sees me for a conceited fraud, a pre-
tentious amateur who gives himself airs.
Anything, anything would be better than
that."

" Then don't go back. Stay here, take
lessons."

" And be in the end—what ? Still third-
rate, still an amateur. I haven't the physical
strength to work hard. Whichever way I
turn I'm caught. But if only people would
believe that I was innocent, that I didn't
know."

" Think of all the pleasure you have given
-Doon. They have spoken about you to me
often. Believe me, they think you great.
There is no conspiracy to deceive you. You
must go back to them, you must play for
them again."

He shook his head.

" Never. You don't know my story—my
father's story. I have always tried to be
perfectly honest, never like him. I, a bigger
deceiver than ever he was. I shall go back—
but I shall never play again."

" Do you think you will be able to keep
that vow ? "

" I shall tell them I cannot play."

" They will force you to play."

" They can never force me to believe in myself again."

" But they will make you play."

Again he shook his head.

" Never. I shall prove to them that I can't play."

" That will be impossible."

" No, quite easy."

" What do you mean ? "

" I shall maim myself, shoot off a finger."

She caught his hands.

" You are mad, you must never do that. It would be wicked. It is a sin even to speak of doing such a thing. You talk of truth, honesty—do you call that honest ? "

" More honest to deceive them once and be done with lies for ever."

" You mustn't, you mustn't."

" I will."

She dropped his hands.

" Why did I bring you to London ? " she moaned.

" Thank God you did. Thank God you taught me the truth."

She sank into a chair.

" It's horrible, you mustn't. Believe in

yourself again, believe they believe, believe *I* believe ! "

To that absurd appeal he made no reply and when she looked at him again a minute later she found he was staring at his hands, stroking the fingers of his right hand gently as if he were bidding them farewell.

1919.

THE END

urse